MW01101405

Nita Mehta's
Vegetarian
Low Calorie Snacks

Vegetarian

100% TRIED & TESTED RECIPES

Nita Mehta
B.Sc. (Home Science), M.Sc. (Food and Nutrition) Gold Medalist

Tanya Mehta

SNAB
Excellence in Books

Nita Mehta's
Vegetarian
Low Calorie Snacks

© Copyright 2005-2010 SNAB Publishers Pvt Ltd

4th Print 2010

ISBN 978-81-7869-090-2

Food Styling and Photography:

Layout and Laser Typesetting :

 National Information Technology Academy
3A/3, Asaf Ali Road
New Delhi-110002
☎ 23252948

Published by :

SNAB Excellence in Books

Publishers Pvt. Ltd.
3A/3 Asaf Ali Road,
New Delhi - 110002
Tel: 23252948, 23250091

Contributing Writers :
Anurag Mehta
Tanya Mehta
Subhash Mehta

Editors :
Sangeeta
Sunita

Editorial and Marketing office:
E-159, Greater Kailash-II, N.Delhi-48
Fax: 91-11-29225218, 29229558
Tel: 91-11-29214011, 29218574
E-Mail: nitamehta@email.com
nitamehta@nitamehta.com
*Website:*http://www.nitamehta.com
Website: http://www.snabindia.com

Distributed by :

NITA MEHTA BOOKS
3A/3, Asaf Ali Road, New Delhi - 02

Distribution Centre:
D16/1, Okhla Industrial Area, Phase-I,
New Delhi-110020
Tel.: 26813199, 26813200
Bhogal: Tel.: 24372279

Printed by :
AEGEAN OFFSET PRINTERS

Recipe Development & Testing:

Nita Mehta Classes/Foods
3A/3, Asaf Ali Road, New Delhi-110002
E-143, Amar Colony, Lajpat Nagar-IV
New Delhi-110024

Rs. 89/-

Picture on Cover :   Soya Sticks 64
                           Light Mustard Dip............................ 98
                           Hari Chutney 99

Picture on Inside front cover :   Baked Yogurt Wheels 72

Picture on page 1 :   Til Waali Fingers 27

Picture on Page 2 :   Chokker Tikki 26

Picture on back cover :   Mushroom-Parsley Bruschetta 82

Picture on page 103 :   Lebanese Smoked Sandwich 92

INTRODUCTION

*N*o more boring fruits or salads or boiled veggies when on a diet. This book has delicious Low Cal Snacks which will satisfy your cravings as well as keep your weight in check. The snacks are delicious and nourishing besides being low in calories.

The recipes are so good that you might feel like treating them to your guests also. With the world getting calorie conscious day-by-day, these recipes will be perfect for your parties as well. Baked chickpea rounds or the steamed triangles or the quick canapes are perfect party snacks.

There is a section on delicious Snacky Dinner, made just with about a teaspoon of oil, using curd and hari chutney. The snacks are all steamed or grilled. Tikkies and kebabs are all made the low fat way. We believe that this book shall prove very useful for the health conscious people, without hampering with the taste of foods.

Nita Mehta

ABOUT THE RECIPES

WHAT'S IN A CUP?

INDIAN CUP
1 teacup = 200 ml liquid
AMERICAN CUP
1 cup = 240 ml liquid (8 oz.)
The recipes in this book were tested with the Indian teacup which holds 200 ml liquid.

Contents

Introduction   6

Indian Snacks & Starters   10

Kurkure Toast   11
Baked Chick Pea Rounds   12
Zucchini Roll Slice   14
Anari Seekhs   16
Hari Idlis   18
Bhel Puri   22
Sprouty Spinach Upma   24
Chokker Tikki   26

Til Waali Fingers   27
Hara Bhara Kebab   28
Instant Dhokla   32
Paneer Tikka   34
Khandavi   36
Kathal Tikka   38
Chatpata Channas   42

Zero Oil Snacks 43

Steamed Triangles 44
Sunset Canapes 46
Cheesy Tomato Boats 47
Crunchy Rounds 48
Mini Suji Oothapam 52

Spiced Babycorns on Bread 54
Dal Seekhs 56
Plain Dosa 58
Khus Khus Paneer Tukda 60
Cornflakes ki Chaat 61

SNACKS
From Around the World 62

Tomato Canapes 63
Soya Sticks 64
Low Fat Crunchy Mini Pizzas 66
Veg Satay 70
Baked Yogurt Wheels 72
Unfried Chilly Potatoes 74

Momos 76
Cocktail Mushrooms 78
Bean Bites 80
Mushroom-Parsley Bruschetta 82
Veggie - Fruity sticks 84

Snacky Dinner 85

Quick Unfried Dahivada 86
Indian Chana Pizza 88
Mango Chutney Footlong 90

Lebanese Smoked Sandwich 92
Mushroom Croustades 96

Chutneys & Dips 97

Meethi Chutney 98
Light Mustard Dip 98
Hari Chutney 99

Lahsun ki Chutney 100
Dahi Poodina Chutney 101
Minty Strawberry Dip 102

INDIAN
Snacks & Starters

Kurkure Toast

Serves 6   *cal/portion 69*

75 gm paneer - crumbled (¾ cup)
2 tbsp suji (semolina), ½ tsp rai (small brown mustard seeds)
½ tsp salt, or to taste, ¼ tsp pepper, or to taste
½ onion - very finely chopped, 2 tbsp curry leaves
½ tomato - cut into half, deseeded and chopped finely
3 bread slices - toasted in a toaster
3 tsp oil to shallow fry

1. Mix paneer with suji, salt and pepper.
2. Add onion, curry leaves and tomato.
3. Spread paneer mixture carefully on toasted bread, keeping edges neat.
4. Sprinkle some rai over the paneer mixture, pressing down gently.
5. Heat 1 tsp oil in a non stick pan. Add a slice of bread with topping side down. Cook until the topping turns golden brown and crisp.
6. Add a little more oil for the next slice if required. Cut each slice into 4 pieces and serve hot.

Baked Chick pea Rounds

Picture on page 93   *Makes* 12   *cal/portion* 43

1 cup chickpeas (kabuli channa)
1 tsp ginger -garlic paste (3-4 flakes of garlic & ½" piece of ginger - crushed to a paste)
2 tbsp chopped coriander leaves
½ tsp salt, or to taste, some black pepper to taste
1 green chilli - very finely chopped
2+2 tbsp curd (thick)
1 tsp dry mint (dry poodina)
½ cup dry bread crumbs

FILLING
2 tbsp grated cottage cheese (paneer)
2 tbsp grated cheese
¼ tsp salt, or to taste

1. Mix paneer and grated cheese with salt. Keep aside.
2. Soak channa overnight. Drain water.
3. Add enough water to cover the channas and ½ tsp salt.
4. Pressure cook channas for 10 minutes or till soft. Remove from fire. Drain. Let it cool. Mash it finely with a potato masher or a kadchi.
5. Add ginger-garlic paste, chopped chilli, coriander, salt, pepper and 2 tbsp of curd and mix lightly with hands.
6. Divide the mixture into 12 equal balls.
7. Stuff each with 1 tsp of filling (paneer cheese mixture). Cover the filling to form a flat round cutlet.
8. Mix 2 tbsp curd with mint and spread this over the round cutlets. Sprinkle bread crumbs well to coat on all the sides.
9. Place on a greased baking tray or a rack covered with foil. Bake at 180°C for 25-30 minutes or until done. Serve garnished with capsicum strips (optional).

Zucchini roll Slice

Serves 8   *cal/portion 83*

ROLLS

4 zucchini or 4 big tori (500 gm) - peeled and grated (2¼ cups)

4 tbsp wheat flour (atta)

2- 3 tbsp gram flour (besan)

4 tbsp semolina (suji)

1 tbsp yoghurt (dahi)

1 green chilli - chopped

a pinch of asafoetida (hing)

¾ tsp salt & ¼ tsp pepper or to taste

1 tbsp chopped coriander leaves

1 tsp dry mint (sookha poodina)

1 tsp lemon juice

1 tsp sugar

1 tsp coriander seeds (saboot dhania) & 1 tsp aniseeds (saunf) - crushed

TO TEMPER
1 tsp oil
½ tsp mustard seeds (rai)
1 tsp carom seeds (ajwain)

1. Grate zucchinis or tori. Squeeze lightly to discard excess water.
2. Crush coriander seeds and saunf together on a chakla belan.
3. Now add all other ingredients of the rolls. Mix well. Add a little more besan if required to bind the mixture. Make 3" long rolls.
4. Now boil water in a deep pan (patila). Grease a stainless steel strainer (channi). Arrange all zuchini rolls over this strainer. Place this strainer on the pan of boiling water. Cover with a lid.
5. Steam for 20 minutes on medium heat, remove the lid and check with a sharp knife. If done, the mixture will not stick to the knife.
6. Let it cool. Now cut rolls into small slices. Keep aside.
7. At serving time, to temper, heat 1 tsp oil. Put rai and ajwain.
8. When they crackle, put zucchini slices. Mix well for few seconds till they get hot. Serve.

Anari Seekhs

Serves 8-10   *cal/portion 94*

¼ cup anaar ke dane (fresh pomegranate seeds)
1 tbsp oil, 3 tbsp thick curd, approx.

BOIL TOGETHER
1 cup kale channe (black chickpeas), ½ cup channe ki dal (split gram)

ADD TO GROUND CHANA MIX
2 green chillies - chopped finely
2 onions - chopped finely
1" piece ginger and 4-5 flakes garlic - crushed or 1 tbsp ginger-garlic paste
1¼ tsp salt, ½ tsp garam masala, ½ tsp amchoor (dried mango powder)

CRUSH TOGETHER
¼ tsp jeera (cumin seeds), seeds of 2 moti illaichi (brown cardamoms)
3-4 laung (cloves) - crushed, 3-4 saboot kali mirch (peppercorns)

BASTING (POURING ON KEBABS)
3 tbsp milk

1. Soak kale chaane and chaane ki dal in some water for 1 hour. Drain water. Pressure cook Chanas and dal with 1½ cups water. After the first whistle, keep cooker on slow fire for 15 minutes. Remove from fire.
2. After the pressure drops down, strain Chanas. Discard water.
3. Divide boiled Chana mixture into 2 portions. Grind one portion in a grinder just for few seconds. Do not make it a smooth paste. Let it be rough. Grind the left over Chanas also in the same way. Mix all together. (Grinding small quantities of Chana at one time is better).
4. Add green chillies, onions, ginger-garlic paste, salt, garam masala and amchoor to Chana paste.
5. Crush jeera, moti illaichi, laung and saboot kali mirch. Mix.
6. Heat 1 tbsp oil in pan, add Chana mixture. Cook for 3-4 minutes.
7. Remove from fire. Add anaar ke daane. Mix well. Add curd to bind the mixture properly.
8. Check salt and add more salt, if required. Make small seekhs.
9. Grill at 230°C for about 10 minutes. Baste (brush) some milk on each seekh to keep them moist. Grill again for 10 minutes or till done. Serve hot with mint chutney.

Hari Idlis

Delicious green paalak idlis. Tastes good even without sambhar & chutney.

Picture on facing page　　　　Serves 12　　　　*cal/portion 46*

1 packet (200 gm) ready-made idli mix
1½ cups chopped spinach leaves (palak ke patte)
2-3 green chillies - deseeded & chopped

TOPPING
2 cups fresh curd - beat well till smooth
½ tsp salt

TEMPERING (TADKA)
1 tbsp oil
1 tsp rai (small brown mustard seeds), ½ tsp jeera (cumin seeds)
2 green chillies - chopped
1 small tomato - chopped finely
20-30 curry leaves (curry patta)

1. Mix the idli mix according to the instructions on the packet.
2. Grind the chopped spinach and green chillies in a mixer to a smooth puree or a paste with 1-2 tbsp water.
3. Add the spinach paste to the idli mixture. Add ¼ tsp salt to it.
4. Grease a mini idli mould. Put a little batter in each cup. Steam for 14-15 minutes on medium flame till a knife inserted in the idli comes out clean. If a mini mould is not available, make small flat idlis by putting a little less batter in the normal idli mould.

5. Place the steamed idlis in a large bowl.
6. Beat the curd with salt till smooth. Pour the curd over the idlis in the bowl. Mix gently. Keep aside for 10-15 minutes.
7. Transfer the idlis to a flat serving platter or a shallow dish.
8. Heat 1 tbsp oil. Add rai and jeera. When jeera turns golden, add green chillies, tomato and curry leaves. Stir to mix all ingredients and immediately pour over the idlis covered with curd. Serve.

◁ *Bhel Puri : Recipe on page 22*

Bhel Puri

Picture on page 20   *Serves 3- 4*   *cal/portion 30*

2 cups murmura (puffed rice)
1 small onion - chopped
1 small potato - boiled & chopped
2 tbsp hari chutney
3 tbsp meethi chutney (see page 61)
1 tbsp red garlic chutney (see page 23)
2 tsp peanuts (moongphali) - split into two pieces
2-3 papadis - roughly crushed or 1 papad - roasted on a naked flame and
roughly crushed
1-2 green chillies - chopped finely
½ tsp chaat masala, ¼ tsp black salt (sanchal)
juice of ½ lemon

GARNISH
2 tbsp chopped coriander

1. Dry roast the murmura (puffed rice) in a kadhai for 10 minutes on medium flame, stirring continuously. This makes the murmura crunchy and crisp.
2. Combine all the ingredients in a large bowl with the roasted murmuras. Mix well with a tablespoon.
3. Serve immediately garnished with coriander.

Red chutney:

Soak peeled flakes of 1 whole pod garlic with 6-8 dried red chillies in 1 cup warm water for 15 minutes. Drain and blend them with 1 tbsp of vinegar to a paste. Add a little water if required for grinding. Add salt to taste.

Sprouty spinach Upma

Serves 6-8   *cal/portion 77*

1 cup moong bean sprouts
4 tomatoes - remove skin by putting in hot water (blanch) & chop finely
2 green chillies - deseeded and chopped
1 cup chopped spinach (palak)
¾ cup suji (semolina)
1½ cups water
4 tsp oil
1 tsp rai (brown mustard seeds)
2 tsp salt, or to taste
½ tsp freshly ground black peppercorns (saboot kali mirch)
juice of ½ lemon

1. Dry roast the suji in a kadhai till it just starts to change colour and becomes fragrant. Keep aside.
2. In a clean kadhai, heat oil. Add rai.
3. When it splutters, and blanched and chopped tomatoes and green chillies. Saute for 2 minutes.
4. To this add sprouts & cook for 2 minutes.
5. Add spinach, salt & crushed peppercorns and cook for 5 minutes. Stir on low heat.
6. Add water and bring to a boil.
7. Add lemon juice.
8. Add suji, stirring continuously and cook till dry. Serve hot.

Chokker Tikki

A good way of having wheat bran, which is the fibrous portion of wheat.
Picture on page 2   Makes 10   cal/portion 30

1 cup (40 gm) chokker (wheat bran)
½ cup grated cauliflower, ½ cup finely chopped paalak (spinach)
1 carrot - grated, 1 potato - boiled, peeled and grated (¾ cups)
1 green chilli - chopped, 2 tbsp green coriander - chopped
¾ tsp salt, ½ tsp black pepper powder, ½ tsp chat masala
1 tsp lemon juice, seeds of 2 chhoti illaichi (green cardamom) - crushed
½ tsp honey
1-2 tbsp curd, approx., 1 tsp oil to brush the pan

1. Mix together chokker with all ingredients except oil and curd.

2. Add enough curd to chokker mixture, to bind the mixture into tikkis.

3. Heat a nonstick frying pan, brush with a little oil and brown the tikkis on both sides on medium heat. Serve hot with hari chutney.

Til waali Fingers

cal/portion 45   *Serves 6*   *Picture on page 1*

4 slices of brown bread
1 tsp white sesame seeds (safed til) or kale til (black sesame seeds)

MIX TOGETHER
2 boiled potatoes - grated (1 cup), 1 tsp tomato sauce
½ onion - very finely chopped, ½ tomato - deseeded and very finely chopped
1 green chilli - deseeded and finely chopped
2 tbsp chopped hara dhania (fresh coriander)
¾ tsp salt, ¼ tsp pepper and ½ tsp chat masala, or to taste

1. Mix all the ingredients written under mix together in a bowl. Divide into 4 portions.
2. Spread each portion of the potato mixture on one bread. Repeat with the remaining bread slices and potato portions.
3. Sprinkle some sesame seeds. Grill in an oven till the toast turns crisp.
4. Cut each slice into 3 long fingers and serve hot.

Hara bhara Kebab

Picture on facing page   *Serves* 12   *cal/portion* 113

1 bundle (600 gm) spinach - only leaves, chopped very finely
1 cup channe ki dal (split gram), 1 tsp oil
3 slices bread - broken into pieces and churned in a mixer to get fresh crumbs
3 tbsp cornflour
2 green chillies - chopped finely
½ tsp red chilli powder, ½ tsp garam masala, ¾ tsp salt or to taste
½ tsp amchoor (dried mango powder)
½ cup grated paneer (50 gm)
¼ cup chopped green coriander

CRUSH TOGETHER
½ tsp jeera, seeds of 2 moti illaichi, 3-4 saboot kali mirch, 2-3 laung

1. Crush jeera, seeds of moti illaichi, kali mirch and laung together.
2. Clean, wash dal. Pressure cook dal with the above crushed spices, ½ tsp salt and 2 cups water. After the first whistle, keep the cooker on slow fire for 15 minutes. Remove from fire and keep aside. *Contd...*

3. After the pressure drops down, mash the hot dal with a karchhi or a potato masher. If there is any water, mash the dal on fire and dry the dal as well while you are mashing it. Remove from fire.
4. Discard stems of spinach and chop leaves very finely. Wash in several changes of water. Leave the chopped spinach in the strainer for 15 minutes so that the water drains out.
5. Heat 1 tsp oil in a nonstick pan or kadhai. Squeeze and add spinach. Stir for 8-10 minutes till spinach is absolutely dry.
6. Add paneer and coriander. Cook for 1 minute. Remove from fire and keep aside.

7. Mix dal with fresh bread crumbs, cornflour, spinach-paneer, green chillies, salt and masalas. Make small balls. Flatten slightly.
8. Cook them on a tawa with just 1 tsp oil till brown on both sides. When done shift them on the sides of the tawa so that they turn crisp while more kebabs can be added in the centre of the tawa. Remove the kebabs on paper napkins.

◁ *Instant Dhokla : Recipe on page 32*

Instant Dhokla

This light Gujarati snack is quick to make in a microwave.

Yellow dhokla prepared instantly from besan, eno fruit salt and soda-bi-carb.

Picture on page 30   *Serves 6- 8*   *cal/portion 105*

1½ cups besan (gram flour)
1 cup water, 1 tbsp oil
½ tsp haldi (turmeric)
1 tsp salt, 1 tsp sugar
1 tsp green chilli paste (crush 2-3 chillies to a paste)
1 tsp ginger paste (½" piece of ginger crushed to a paste)
1½ tsp eno fruit salt
¼ tsp soda-bi-carb (mitha soda), 2 tsp lemon juice

TEMPERING
1 tsp oil, 2-3 green chillies - slit into long pieces
1 tsp rai (mustard seeds)
¾ cup water, 1 tbsp sugar
¼ cup white vinegar

1. Grease a 7" diameter round, flat dish with oil. Keep aside.
2. Sift besan through sieve to make it light and free of any lumps.
3. Mix besan, water, oil, haldi, salt, sugar, chilli paste, ginger paste and water to a smooth batter.
4. Add eno fruit salt and soda-bi-carb to the batter and pour lemon juice over it. Beat well for a few seconds.
5. Immediately pour this mixture in the greased dish. Steam for 12-13 minutes on medium heat, till the back of a spoon inserted in the dhokla comes out clean. OR Microwave uncovered for 6 minutes. Remove from oven and keep aside.
6. To temper, microwave oil, green chillies, rai, water, sugar and vinegar for 4½ minutes. Pour over the dhokla and wait for ½ hour to absorb it and to turn soft.
7. Cool and cut into 1" pieces.
8. Sprinkle chopped coriander. Serve.

Paneer Tikka

Picture on page 49   *Serves 4-6*   *cal/portion 17*

300 gm paneer - cut into 1½" pieces of 1" thickness
1 large capsicum - deseeded and cut into 1" pieces (12 pieces)
1 onion - cut into 4 pieces and then separated

MARINADE

¾ cup dahi (yogurt) - hang in a muslin cloth for 15 minutes
1" piece ginger, 5-6 flakes garlic - crushed to a paste (2 tsp ginger - garlic paste)
1½ tbsp oil, 1 tbsp (level) cornflour
½ tsp amchoor, ¾ tsp salt, or to taste, ½ tsp chaat masala
1 tbsp tandoori masala or ¾ tsp garam masala
a few drops of orange colour or a pinch of haldi (turmeric)

1. Hang yogurt in a muslin cloth (mal-mal ka kapda) for 15 minutes.
2. Transfer the hung yogurt to a flat bowl. Beat till smooth.
3. Add ginger-garlic paste, 1½ tbsp oil, 1 tbsp cornflour, amchoor, salt, chaat masala, tandoori masala and colour or haldi to the paste.
4. Add paneer to the marinade. Mix well so that all pieces of paneer get well coated with the marinade on all the sides.

5. Rub some oil over the grill of the oven or wire rack of a gas tandoor. Place paneer on the greased wire rack or grill of the oven.

6. Arrange paneer on greased rack. After arranging all the paneer pieces on the wire rack, put the capsicum and onions - both together in the left over marinade in which paneer was kept. Mix well to coat the vegetables with the marinade. Leave the vegetables in the bowl itself.

7. About ½ hour before serving, put the paneer pieces placed on the wire rack in the hot oven at about 180°C. Bake/grill for 15 minutes or till almost done. Bake/grill the paneer till it gets slightly dry.

8. Spoon some drops of oil or melted butter on the paneer pieces. Now remove the vegetables from the bowl and put them also in the oven on the sides of the paneer. Grill everything together for another 10 minutes. The vegetables should not be in the oven for too long.

9. Remove from the oven. Transfer to a serving platter. If you like microwave for 1 minute to further soften the paneer. Serve immediately (really hot), sprinkled with some lemon juice and chaat masala.

Khandavi

A very popular snack of Western India. Strips of cooked gram flour are rolled into a delicious snack. The filling makes all the difference.

Picture on page 40   *Serves 8*   *cal/portion 56*

½ cup besan (gram flour)
½ cup curd (not sour) mixed with 1 cup water to get 1½ cups butter milk (lassi)
¼ tsp haldi (turmeric powder), ¼ tsp jeera powder (ground cumin seeds)
½ tsp dhania powder, a pinch of hing (asafoetida) powder, 1 tsp salt
½" piece ginger and 1-2 green chillies - grind to a paste together

FILLING

½ tbsp oil, ½ tsp rai (mustard seeds), 1 tbsp grated fresh coconut
2 tbsp grated carrot (gajar), 1 tsp kishmish (raisins) - chopped
1 tbsp chopped coriander, 2 pinches salt

CHOWNK (TEMPERING)

½ tbsp oil, ½ tsp rai (small, brown mustard seeds)
2-3 green chillies - cut into thin long pieces, a few coriander leaves

1. Mix besan with 1½ cups buttermilk till smooth. Add haldi, jeera powder, dhania powder, hing, salt and ginger-green chilli paste.
2. Spread a cling film (plastic sheet) on the backside of a big tray.
3. Keep the mixture on low heat in a non stick pan. Cook this mixture for about 25 minutes, stirring, till the mixture becomes very thick and translucent. Drop 1 tsp mixture on the tray and spread. Let it cool for a while and check if it comes out easily. If it does, remove from fire, otherwise cook for another 5 minutes. Remove from fire.
4. While the mixture is still hot, quickly spread some mixture as thinly & evenly as possible on the cling film. Level it with a knife. Keep aside.
5. For the filling, heat oil. Add rai. After it crackles, add coconut, carrot, kishmish and chopped coriander. Add salt. Mix. Remove from fire.
6. After the besan mixture cools, neaten the rectangle by cutting the edges straight with a knife. Cut widthwise into 2" wide strips.
7. Put 1 tsp filling at one end of a strip. Roll each strip, loosening with a knife initially, to get small cylinders. Keep in a serving plate.
8. Heat ½ tbsp oil. Add rai. When rai splutters, add green chillies. Remove from fire and pour the oil on the khandavis. Garnish with coriander.

Kathal Tikka

Picture on facing page   *Serves 6-8*   *cal/portion 75*

300 gms of kathal (jack fruit), a pinch of haldi
2 tbsp milk mixed with 1 tsp oil - to baste (pour on the tikka)

MARINADE

1 cup thick curd - hang in a muslin cloth for 30 minutes
1 tbsp tandoori masala
1 tbsp ginger paste (1" piece of ginger - crushed to a paste)
¼ tsp red chilli powder, ¾ tsp salt, 1 tbsp oil
a pinch of tandoori colour or haldi

CRUSH TOGETHER TO A ROUGH POWDER

½ tsp bhuna jeera (roasted cumin)
seeds of 2 chhoti illaichi (green cardamom)
3-4 saboot kali mirch (peppercorns)
2-3 blades/pinches of javitri (mace)

Contd...

1. Hang curd in a muslin cloth for ½ hour.
2. Rub oil on your hands. Cut the whole big piece of kathal from the middle into two pieces. Remove skin. Cut widthwise from the centre of each piece. This way you get two big strips of kathal. Now further divide each strip into smaller pieces about 1" thickness, carefully to keep the shreds of the piece together. Then further divide into ½" thick pieces.
3. Boil 7-8 cups of water with 2 tsp salt and a pinch of haldi. Add kathal and boil for 10 minutes till crisp-tender. Keep aside.
4. Grind or crush bhuna jeera, seeds of chhoti illaichi, saboot kali mirch and 2-3 pinches of javitri to a rough powder.
5. Mix all the ingredients of the marinade and freshly ground chhoti illaichi-kali mirch powder. Mix in kathal. Let it marinate for an hour in the refrigerator.
6. Place the tikkas on a greased wire rack (jaali) or on a grill rack. Bake at 180°C for 15 minutes or till the coating gets slightly dry.
7. Spoon some oil or melted butter on it (baste) and grill further for 10 minutes till coating turns absolutely dry. Sprinkle some chaat masala.
8. Serve hot with poodina chutney.

◅ *Khandavi : Recipe on page 36*

Chatpata Channas

Serves 3-4   *cal/portion* 122

1 cup kabuli channas (white chickpeas) - soaked overnight, 1 tsp oil
½ tsp sarson (mustard seeds)
1 tsp urad dal - soaked for 15 minutes
a pinch of hing (asafoetida), a few curry leaves (curry patta)
½ tsp red chilli powder
2-3 green chillies - chopped, 1" piece ginger - shredded, 2 tsp lemon juice
2 tbsp chopped kairi (raw mango) - cut into tiny pieces or ½ tsp amchoor
salt to taste, 2 tbsp chopped coriander

1. Drain the soaked channas. Pressure cook channas with 2 cups water and 1 tsp salt to give 1 whistle. Keep on low heat for 10-12 minutes.
2. Heat 1 tsp oil on low heat. Add sarson. When it splutters, add urad dal, hing and curry leaves. Fry for 2 minutes till dal turns brown.
3. Add red chilli powder. Add cooked channas, green chillies and ginger to it. Add mango pieces and salt to taste. Mix well. Dry the liquid, if any, on fire. Add lemon juice. Garnish with coriander leaves.
4. Serve hot or cold.

Zero Oil Snacks

Steamed Triangles

Serves 6   *cal/portion 84*

1 cup semolina (sooji) - roasted
¾ tsp salt
1 cup dahi (curd)
½ tsp oregano
1 tbsp eno fruit salt
½ carrot (gajar)- grated
2-3 tbsp chopped capsicums
4 tbsp hari chutney
½ tsp sugar
1 tsp oil

1. Roast semolina in a kadhai, stirring continuously. Cool.
2. Add salt, curd and oregano. Mix well to get a thick batter.
3. Boil 3 glasses of water in a deep pan (patila). Mix eno with sooji batter and transfer half of the batter to a greased thali to get ½" thick layer.

4. Sprinkle most of the grated carrot mixture and chopped capsicum over it. Then sprinkle drops of hari chutney with a spoon all over.

5. Pour the rest of sooji mixture.
6. Top with the remaining grated carrot and capsicum.
7. Steam for 15-20 minutes and check with a knife in the centre. If it comes out clean it is done. Take out and cut into 2" triangles or square pieces.

Sunset Canapes

Makes 10-12　　　　　　　*cal/portion 40*

5-6 slices bread
1 small cucumber - cut into thin slices without peeling and dipped for 30 minutes
in ½ cup vinegar to which 1 tsp sugar and 1 tsp salt has been mixed
1 orange, a few fresh or tinned cherry
cheese spread, some bhuna jeera or crushed black pepper
some chaat masala

1. Toast bread slices till crisp. With a cutter or a sharp lid, cut out small rounds (about 1½" diameter) of the each bread or cut sides and then into 2 rectangles.

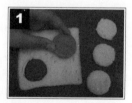

2. Spread some cheese spread. Sprinkle some bhuna jeera or pepper.

3. Place a pickled cucumber slice. Open an orange segment, cut into half and place it on the side of kheera and top with a cherry.

4. Sprinkle some chaat masala and serve.

Cheesy tomato Boats

cal/portion 11

Serves 4

2 firm big, longish tomatoes
50 gms paneer - grated (4 tbsp)
1 tbsp chopped coriander
1 tsp finely chopped onion, optional
½" piece of ginger - grated, 1 tsp lemon juice
3-4 saboot kali mirch (peppercorns) - crushed
¼ tsp salt, or to taste

TO GARNISH
a few olives, optional, some parsley or coriander

1. Cut a very thin slice from the top of each tomato. Scoop out the pulp from tomatoes with a knife or a scooper leaving the walls intact. Rub some salt inside and keep them inverted for a few minutes.
2. Gently mix grated paneer with all the other ingredients.
3. Stuff into the tomato shells and press well. Cut each tomato into 4 pieces lengthwise, with a sharp knife.
4. Garnish each boat with a slice of olive & a coriander or parsley leaf.

Crunchy Rounds

cal/portion   78   *Serves 6*

6 bread slices
1 large potato - boiled and grated
1 small onion - chopped finely
1 carrot (gajar) - grated
1 capsicum - chopped very finely (diced)
2 tsp soya sauce
2 tsp tomato sauce
¾ tsp salt, or to taste
½ tsp pepper (kalimirch)
¼ tsp red chilli powder
2 tsp sesame seeds (til) - to sprinkle

1. In a non stick pan add onions with ¼ cup water. Cook till onions turn soft and the water dries.

Contd...

Paneer Tikka : Recipe on page 34 ➤

2. Add vegetables. Cook for 2 minutes on low flame.
3. Reduce heat. Add potatoes, soya sauce, tomato sauce, salt, pepper and red chilli powder. Cook for 2-3 minutes. Keep aside.
4. With a biscuit cutter or a sharp lid, cut out small rounds (about 1½" diameter) of the bread.
5. Spread some potato mixture in a slight heap on the round piece of bread, leaving the edges. Press.
6. Sprinkle sesame seeds. Press. Place on a grill rack.
7. Bake at 180°C for 8 minutes or till bread turns crisp from the under side. Serve, dotted with chilli-garlic or masala chilli tomato sauce.

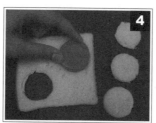

Final Recipe

◁ *Mini Suji Oothapam : Recipe on page 52*

Mini suji Oothapam

These thick South Indian pancakes can be prepared without having to wait for the batter to ferment. The sour curd and soda bi carb take care of the lightness without fermentation.

Picture on page 50   *Makes 6-8*   *cal/portion 87*

BATTER
1½ cups rava or moti suji (coarse semolina)
1½ cups sour curd (khatti dahi), ¾ cup water
¼ tsp mitha soda (soda-bi-carb), 1 tsp salt
¼ tsp hing (asafoetida powder)

TOPPING
1-2 green chillies - chopped
a few curry leaves - chopped
2 onions - chopped
2 tomatoes - chopped
1 carrot - grated
salt to taste

1. Mix all ingredients of the batter together.
2. Add enough water to the batter to get a thick pouring consistency. Beat well.
3. Keep the batter aside for ½ hour.
4. At serving time, add mitha soda and mix well.
5. Mix all ingredients of the topping together. Keep aside.
6. Heat a non stick tawa. Wipe with a potato or onion cut into half.
7. Mix the batter well. Keeping the gas on low flame, pour 1 small karchhi (2 tbsp) of batter on it. Spread the batter a little with the back of the karchhi, keeping it slightly thick. Make small oothapams.

8. After 2 minutes, sprinkle a little topping on it. Press the topping a little with a potato masher.
9. After the underside is cooked, turn the side carefully.
10. Remove from tawa after the other side also gets cooked and the onions turn a little brown.
11. Serve hot with tomato ketchup.

Spiced babycorns on Bread

cal/portion 56   *Serves 10-12*

1 French Loaf or garlic bread - cut into ¼" thick diagonal slices
50 gm paneer (2" cube) - grated
2 tbsp chopped mint (poodina)

BABY CORN TOPPING

150 gm baby corns - sliced into rounds (1½ cups)
2 tsp vinegar, 2 tsp soya sauce, 1 tsp red chilli sauce
2 tbsp cornflour dissolved in ½ cup water
½ tsp salt, ½ tsp pepper

TOMATO SPREAD

6-8 flakes garlic - crushed
¼ tsp red chilli powder
½ cup ready made tomato puree
2 tbsp tomato sauce
1 tsp oregano (dried) or ½ tsp ajwain
½ tsp salt and ½ tsp pepper to taste

1. To prepare the spread, mix all the ingredients and cook on low flame for about 5 minutes, till thick. Keep aside.
2. To prepare the topping, mix all ingredients, except the baby corns in a heavy bottomed pan or kadhai and then add the sliced baby corns. Keep on fire and cook on low flame, stirring continuously till the sauce coats the baby corns and they get cooked a little.
3. Spread some tomato spread on the slices. Arrange some baby corns in sauce. Press.
4. Grate some paneer finely over it. Sprinkle some mint, crushed peppercorns and some salt on the paneer.
5. To serve, place pieces on a grill rack. Bake at 200°C for 7-8 minutes till a little crisp. Do not over cook otherwise they turn too hard.

Note: If baby corns are not available, cooked or tinned corn kernels may be substituted.

Dal Seekhs

Serves 6-8

BOIL TOGETHER
1½ cups channe ki dal (split gram)
1 tsp salt, ¼ tsp jeera (cumin seeds)
seeds of 2 moti illaichi (brown cardamom) - crushed
3-4 laung (cloves) - crushed
3-4 saboot kali mirch (peppercorns) - crushed
1" piece ginger and 4-5 flakes garlic - crushed or 1 tbsp ginger-garlic paste
2½ cups water

OTHER INGREDIENTS
2 green chillies - chopped finely
2 onions - chopped finely
4-5 tbsp chopped poodina (mint)
½ tsp garam masala, ½ tsp amchoor (dried mango powder)

1. Clean, wash dal. Pressure cook dal with salt, jeera, crushed seeds of moti illaichi, crushed laung, crushed saboot kali mirch, ginger-garlic paste and water.
2. After the first whistle, keep the cooker on slow fire for 15 minutes.
3. After the pressure drops down, mash the hot dal with a karchhi. If there is any water, mash the dal on fire and dry the dal as well while you are mashing it. Remove from fire.
4. Add all other ingredients to the mashed dal.
5. Check salt and add more salt, if required. Make small seekhs. Place on a grill rack.
6. Bake at 230°C for about 20 minutes till done. Serve hot with mint chutney.

Final Recipe

Plain Dosa

cal/portion 104   *Makes about 15*

BATTER

2 cups sela or ushna chaawal (parboiled) rice of ordinary quality
1 cup permal chaawal (ordinary quality rice)
1 cup dhuli urad dal (split black gram dal)
2 tsp methi dana (fenugreek seeds), 2 tsp salt

1. To prepare the batter, soak both the rice, dal & fenugreek seeds together in a pan for at least 6 hours. Grind together finely to a paste, using some of the water in which it was soaked. Add more water to the paste, if required, to get a paste of medium pouring consistency. Add salt. Mix.

2. Keep aside for 12 hours or overnight in a warm place, to get fermented. After fermentation, the batter rises a little and smells sour.

3. To prepare the dosa, mix the batter nicely with a karchhi.

4. Heat a non stick tawa on medium flame. Put a few drops of oil and rub the oil with a cut onion half to wipe off the oil.
5. Remove the pan from fire and pour 1 heaped karchhi of batter. Spread quickly, but lightly. Return to fire. Cook till the dosa get a little cooked.
6. After golden brown spots appear, gently loosen the sides and the bottom.
7. Fold over from both sides. Remove from tawa. Serve immediately with hari chutney.

Khus khus paneer Tukda

cal/portion 43   Serves 6

400 gm paneer - cut into ½" thick, 1½ x 3/4" pieces
2 tbsp khus khus (poppy seeds), some chat masala to sprinkle

GREEN PASTE

1 cup fresh coriander - chopped along with stems, ½ cup chopped poodina (mint)
1 onion - chopped, 3-4 green chillies
a pinch of hing (asafoetida), ½ tsp jeera (cumin seeds)
2 tsp amchoor (approx.), ½ tsp salt

1. Prepare the green paste by grinding all ingredients together.
2. Make a slit half way in the paneer slice and fill some paste in between. Smear some paste all over the paneer pieces.
3. Press over khus spread out in a plate. Turn the paneer piece and coat the other side of the paneer piece also with some khus khus.
4. Arrange the paneer pieces on a greased grill tray. Put under a hot grill for 15 minutes or bake at 220°C till golden. Serve immediately, sprinkled with chaat masala.

Cornflakes ki Chaat

cal/portion 47   *Serves 6*

1½ cups cornflakes (Kellog's)
1 boiled potato - finely chopped
¼ cup boiled kabuli or kaala channas (black chickpeas)
1 green chilli - chopped, 2 tbsp hara dhania - chopped, 1 tomato - chopped finely
some bhuna jeera powder

MEETHI CHUTNEY
1 tbsp amchoor, 2 tbsp sugar, ¼ cup water
½ tsp salt ½ tsp red chilli powder & ½ tsp bhuna jeera

1. For chutney, mix all ingredients. Boil. Cook for a few minutes, stirring continuously, till slightly thick. Remove from fire and keep aside.
2. Mix potato, channa, chilli, dhania, tomato with chutney in a big bowl.
3. Just at the time of serving, add the cornflakes. Quickly mix lightly.
4. Sprinkle some bhuna jeera (roasted cumin) powder. Serve immediately otherwise it tends to become soggy.

SNACKS
From Around the World

Tomato Canapes

Makes a good cocktail sandwich snack for a party.

cal/portion 27   *Makes 8 small pieces*

2 slices of bread - toasted in a toaster
1 spring onion (hara pyaz) - chop only the greens
1 cheese cube - chopped into 8 small pieces

PASTE
1 tbsp chilli garlic sauce (maggi)
2 tbsp tomato ketchup, 1 tbsp curd, ¼ tsp soya sauce
¼ tsp oregano, ¼ tsp salt

1. Blend all ingredients of the paste in a grinder till smooth.
2. Toast the bread slices in a toaster. Cut into 4 square pieces. Spread the tomato spread on each piece. Cover with greens of spring onion and top in the centre with a tiny piece of cheese. Sprinkle pepper. Serve immediately at room temperature.

Soya Sticks

Soya beans are one of the richest sources of lecithin, which are great emulsifiers of fat.

Picture on cover   Serves 6   *cal/portion* 53

1 cup soya chunks - boiled in water till soft, keep it soaked in warm water for
½ hour - drain and squeeze

1 onion - cut into 8 pieces and separated

1 capsicum - cut into ¾" squares pieces

¼ cup curd (dahi)

1 tsp salt and ½ tsp pepper, or to taste

2 tsp oil

½ tsp ajwain (carom seeds)

1½ tsp garlic paste (4-5 flakes of garlic- crushed to a paste)

½ tsp red chilli powder, 2 tbsp tomato sauce, 1 tsp soya sauce

a few tooth picks

1. Boil nuggets in water till soft. Remove from fire. Cover and keep them soaked in this water for 10-20 minutes. Squeeze well and keep aside.
2. Beat curd till smooth. Add salt and pepper.
3. Marinate the nutri nugget chunks in the curd mixture. Keep aside till serving time.
4. Heat 1 tsp oil in a non stick pan. Reduce flame. Add ajwain and wait for a minute. Add garlic paste. Stir for a few seconds till it changes colour. Remove from heat. Add red chilli powder.
5. Add tomato sauce and soya sauce.
6. Return to fire. Add nuggets along with the curd mixture. Cook till almost dry.
7. Add onion and capsicum squares and saute for 2 minutes. Sprinkle some salt and pepper and mix well till dry. Remove from fire.
8. Thread a onion, then a soya ball and lastly a capsicum piece on the tooth pick. Serve hot.

Low fat crunchy mini Pizzas

Picture on facing page   *Serves 8*   *cal/portion 66*

FOR MINI PIZZA BASES
½ cup luke warm water
½ tsp sugar
1 tsp heaped dried yeast (5 gm)
½ cup milk
½ tbsp oil, ½ tsp salt
1 cup maida (plainflour) mixed with ½ cup atta (whole wheatflour)

OTHER INGREDIENTS
some ketchup to spread on base
1 onion - chopped, 1 small capsicum - chopped
½ cup breadcrumbs (to sprinkle)
½ tbsp cheese spread
a few slices of onion

1. Take warm water in a cup. Feel the water with a finger to check if it is lukewarm. Add yeast. Shake the cup gently to mix the yeast. Cover it

and leave it in a warm place till the granules of the yeast disappear and it becomes frothy. (10-15 minutes). (If it does not swell, discard it).

2. Mix milk, oil, salt and sugar in a pan. Keep aside. When the yeast becomes frothy, heat this milk mixture to make it lukewarm. Add the ready yeast mix to the luke warm milk mixture.

3. Add this yeast and milk mixture to the maida- atta mixture. Knead well to make a smooth dough. Grease a big polythene, brush the dough with a little oil and put it in the polythene. Keep it covered in a warm place to swell for 1 hour or till it is double in size. Now punch it down to its original size, brush with oil and keep it back in the polythene for another 15 minutes or till it swells again.

4. Make 6- 8 balls. Roll into 3" diameter rounds. Prick each base with a fork.

5. Bake in a preheated oven at 180°C/350°F for 8- 10 minutes.

6. Remove from oven, put cheese spread on base and then put ketchup.

7. Give a layer of vegetable filling, sprinkle breadcrumbs and top with an onion slice. Bake till the top becomes golden and crisp. Serve with mustard sauce.

◁ *Veg Satay : Recipe on page 70*

Veg Satay

Vegetable on wooden skewers.

Picture on page 68   *Makes 6 Skewers*   *cal/portion 59*

100 gm tofu or paneer - cubed to get 1½ " squares
6 baby corns, small sized - put in boiling water for 3 minutes and wipe dry
6 mushrooms - trim stalk and keep whole, 1 green capsicum - cut into 1" cubes
6 cherry tomatoes or 1 large, firm tomato cut into 8 pieces and pulp removed

MARINADE

½ tsp salt, ¼-½ tsp red chilli powder
2 tsp brown sugar or gur
2 fresh red chillies - seeded and thinly sliced
3 tbsp coconut milk
½ tsp soya sauce
1" piece of ginger - grated
1 tsp lemon juice, 1 tsp brown or ¾ tsp regular sugar
2 tsp cornflour
8-10 flakes garlic - crushed to a paste
½ tsp jeera powder (ground cumin), ½ tsp dhania powder (coriander powder)

1. Boil 3 cups water in a pan, add babycorn and mushrooms in it. Boil for 2-3 minutes. Remove from fire, strain and refresh in cold water.
2. Mix all ingredients of marinade together. Add tofu or paneer, blanched baby corns, mushrooms and tomatoes. Keep covered for ½ hour or till serving time.
3. Thread a mushroom, then a baby corn, then a cherry tomato or regular tomato piece and lastly a paneer piece onto oiled wooden skewers. Leave behind the marinade. Keep aside.
4. Cook in a preheated oven at 180°C/350°F for 6-7 minutes. Baste (pour) with a spoon the remaining marinade on the sticks and cook for another 2-3 minutes.

Baked yogurt Wheels

Picture on inside front cover   *Serves 4*   cal/portion 75

4 slices of soft fresh bread, 2-3 tbsp milk, 1 tsp ajwain (carom seeds)
4 tbsp moong sprouts, optional
9 paalak (spinach) leaves

FILLING

1 cup curd - hang for 1 hour in a thin muslin cloth and squeeze
½ carrot - grated (½ cup) & squeezed, 1 capsicum - finely chopped (½ cup)
1 green chilli - deseeded & finely chopped
1 tsp salt, ½ tsp crushed peppercorns, ¼ tsp each dhania & red chilli powder
1 tsp tomato ketchup (masala chilli)
½ tsp bhuna jeera powder (roasted cumin powder)

1. Hang curd for 1 hour. Squeeze well to drain out all water. Put the curd in a bowl. Add all other ingredients of the filling to the curd and mix lightly with a fork. Keep filling aside.
2. Cut the sides of a slice, keep it flat on a rolling board.

3. Press, applying pressure with a belan so that holes of the bread close. Keep aside. Similarly roll another slice. (You may microwave the bread slice for a few seconds before rolling.)
4. Keep both the slices slightly overlapping, about ¼" to get a long piece.
5. Press with belan on the joint. Spread spinach leaves (cut stalks completely) on bread.
6. Spread a layer of filling on leaf & empty spaces.
7. Sprinkle some sprouts on the filling. Roll carefully.
8. Seal end by applying some curd. Press well.
9. Brush milk on roll. Spread some ajwain on a plate and roll the bread roll over it. Gently cut each roll into 4-5 pieces to get wheels of about ¾" thickness.
10. At serving time, cover a wire rack of oven with foil. Grease foil lightly. Place wheels standing upright on it. Bake in a hot oven (200°C) for about 10 minutes till edges turn golden. Serve immediately.

Unfried chilly Potatoes

cal/portion 99 Serves 4-6

12-15 baby potatoes or 3 small potatoes - boiled & cut into 4 pieces
1 large capsicum - cut into ½" - ¾" pieces
3-4 flakes garlic - crushed
1 green chilli - deseeded & chopped
¼ tsp red chilli powder
1 tbsp vinegar
2 tsp soya sauce
2 tbsp tomato ketchup
1 tsp red chilli sauce
2-3 tbsp very finely chopped coriander
1 tbsp oil

1. Peel and cut boiled potatoes into 1" pieces.
2. Cut capsicum into ½"- ¾" square pieces.
3. Heat 1 tbsp oil in a wok or a non stick pan. Reduce flame.

74

4. Add garlic & green chillies. Stir.
5. Shut off the fire. Add red chilli powder, vinegar, soya sauce, tomato ketchup and red chilli sauce.
6. Return to fire. Add ¼ tsp salt and add potatoes. Toss well to mix.
7. Add finely chopped coriander.
8. Cook on medium flame for 3-4 minutes, adding 2 tbsp of water so that the sauces do not burn, till potatoes get coated with the sauce.
9. Reduce flame. Add the capsicum. Mix well. Remove from fire after a minute, otherwise the capsicum changes colour.
10. To serve, add a few tbsp water & heat well. Pass a piece of capsicum, keeping the green side up through a toothpick, then pass a piece of potato, keeping the flat side down. Pass another piece of capsicum to sandwich the potato in between the capsicum pieces. Serve hot.

Note: The toothpicks with potato and capsicum can be made in advance and heated at the time of serving in a microwave.

Momos

Makes 12   *cal/portion 67*

DOUGH
1 cup maida (plain flour), 1 tbsp oil, ¼ tsp salt

FILLING
1½ tbsp oil
1 onion - finely chopped, 6 mushrooms - chopped very finely
1 large carrot - very finely chopped or grated
1 tsp ginger-garlic paste, 2 green chillies - finely chopped
2½ cups very finely chopped cabbage (1 small cabbage)
1 tsp salt and ½ tsp pepper powder, or to taste

RED HOT CHUTNEY
4-5 dry Kashmiri red chillies - deseeded and soaked in ¼ cup warm water
6-8 flakes garlic, 1 tsp saboot dhania (coriander seeds)
1 tsp jeera (cumin seeds), ½ tsp salt, 1 tsp sugar
3 tbsp vinegar, ½ tsp soya sauce

1. For the dough, sift maida with salt. Add oil and knead with enough water to make a stiff dough of rolling consistency, as that for puris.
2. Heat oil in the kadhai for the filling. Add chopped onion. Fry till it turns soft. Add mushrooms and cook further for 2 minutes. Add carrot, green chillies & ginger-garlic paste. Mix well and add the cabbage. Stir fry on high flame for 3 minutes. Add salt, pepper to taste. Remove from fire.
3. Make marble sized balls and roll thinly, to make about 5" rounds. Put 1 heaped tbsp of the filling. Pick up the sides into loose folds like frills and keep collecting each fold in the centre, to give a flattened ball (like kachorie) like shape. Make all momos.
4. Place the momos in a greased idli stand and steam it in a pressure cooker with 1 cup water without the whistle for 3-4 minutes.
5. This momo can be had steamed, or it can be baked in the oven at 200°C for 5 minutes till light golden on the edges. Serve with chutney.
6. For the chutney, grind the soaked red chillies along with the water, garlic, dhania, jeera, salt and sugar to a paste. Add soya sauce and vinegar to taste.

Cocktail Mushrooms

Choose big sized mushrooms so that they can be stuffed easily.

Serves 4   *cal/portion 34*

12 fresh mushrooms of a slightly bigger size
juice of ½ lemon

FILLING
½ tbsp oil
2 tbsp finely chopped onion
2 tsp cornflour
slightly less than ½ cup milk (1/3 cup approx.)
¼ tsp salt
¼ tsp pepper

1. Wash mushrooms well.
2. Boil 2 cups water in a small pan with 1 tsp salt and lemon juice.
3. Add the mushrooms. Give one boil. Remove from fire, drain & cool.
4. Gently pull out the stem, loosening from all sides of each mushroom with the help of a knife. Discard stalks. Make a hollow in the cap with the back of a spoon. Keep mushrooms aside.
5. Mix cornflour with milk and keep aside.
6. Heat oil in a small heavy bottomed kadhai. Add chopped onion and stir on low flame for 2-3 minutes till brown. Remove from fire.
7. Add milk mixed with cornflour. Return to fire and cook, stirring till very thick. Add salt and pepper to taste. Remove filling from fire.
8. Cool the filling. Stuff each mushroom with the filling, mounting it slightly.
9. Bake in an oven at 180°C for 10 minutes in a greased oven proof glass dish.
10. Insert a tooth pick and garnish with a coriander leaf.
11. Serve hot on a bed of shredded lettuce or cabbage.

Note: Extra filling can be used as bread spread for a refreshing toasted snack. The msuhroom stalks can be used for making a soup.

Bean Bites

A very simple starter. Biscuits are topped with beans and sour cream.

Serves 8　　　　　*cal/portion 100*

1 packet cream cracker biscuits

or

any other salted biscuits like monacco

BEAN TOPPING

¾ cup of ready-made baked beans (tin), 1 tsp butter
1 tbsp chopped coriander or parsley
2 flakes of garlic, ¼ tsp salt, ¼ tsp pepper to taste
1-2 drops of tabasco sauce (optional)

SOUR CREAM

½ cup thick curd (dahi), ¼ tsp salt
¼ tsp freshly crushed pepper (saboot kali mirch, powdered)
1 green chilli - remove seeds and chop finely, ¼ tsp vinegar

GARNISH

2 tbsp chopped coriander or 1 spring onion - chop green part very finely

1. To prepare the sour cream, hang curd in a muslin cloth for 20 minutes.

2. Beat the hung curd with a wire whisk or fork till smooth. Add salt and pepper to taste. Mix in very finely chopped green chillies and vinegar. Keep aside.

3. For bean topping, put butter in a kadhai, let it melt a little, add garlic and fry till it starts to change colour.

4. Add ready-made beans, coriander, salt and pepper. Cook for 2 minutes. Remove from fire. Add tabasco if using. Keep aside.

5. At serving time, heat the filling and spread 1 heaped teaspoon of it on each cream cracker, leaving the edges clean.

6. Drop ½ tsp of the sour cream in the centre portion. Sprinkle some greens of the spring onion on the sour cream. Serve immediately.

Tip: *½ cup boiled rajmah mixed with ¼ cup tomato sauce and ¼ tsp each of oregano, salt and pepper can be used instead of the ready made baked beans.*

To store beans: *Transfer the left over ready-made baked beans to a steel or plastic container/box. Keep it in freezer compartment of the refrigerator for 1-2 months & use as required.*

Mushroom-parsley Bruschetta

Hot & crisp garlic flavoured bread pieces topped with herbed mushrooms.

Picture on backcover   *Makes 20 pieces*   *cal/portion 78*

TOPPING

200 gm mushrooms - chopped finely
¾ cup chopped fresh parsley
3 tbsp oil, 5 flakes garlic - chopped very finely
1 big onion - chopped very finely
¾ tsp salt & ½ tsp freshly ground peppercorns, or to taste
1 tsp dried oregano

BREAD

a small French bread - cut into slices of ½" thickness, about 18-20 slices

1. Heat oil. Add garlic & onions. Cook for 2 minutes till onions are golden.
2. Add mushrooms and cook for 3 minutes. Add parsley.
3. Add salt, pepper and oregano and mix well. Remove from fire.

4. At serving time, bake the bread slices in a pre-heated oven at 200°C/360°F for 10 minutes till each is lightly toasted and crisp. Alternately, toast the slices on a pan or tawa on low heat till crisp on both sides.
5. Spread 1 heaped tbsp of mushroom mixture (at room temperature) on the toasted slice. Serve immediately.

Variation - Tomato Bruschetta

TOPPING - (mix together and keep aside for at least 30 minutes)
2 tomatoes - pulp removed and chopped finely, 2 tbsp balsqunic vinegance, 6-8 flakes garlic - chopped very finely
1 tbsp fresh basil leaves - chopped, ½ tsp dried oregano, 2-3 tbsp olive oil
½ tsp salt and ½ tsp freshly ground peppercorns, or to taste

1. Cut each tomato into 4 pieces and gently remove all the seeds and pulp. Chop the deseeded tomatoes into very small pieces.
2. Mix all the other ingredients with chopped tomatoes and keep aside at room temperature for at least 30 minutes for the tomatoes to absorb the flavours. Use it on garlic bread instead of the mushroom mixture.

Veggie - fruity sticks

Serves 4-5   *cal/portion 51*

6 thick baby corns - blanched & cut into half to get 2 smaller pieces
1 tbsp vinegar, 1 tbsp olive oil
1 tbsp finely chopped coriander or parsley
3 cubes of cheddar cheese (Britannia) - each cut into 4 pieces
2 rings tinned or fresh pineapple rings - cut into 1" wedges
a few big mint leaves - dipped in ice cold water for 30 minutes
12-15 tinned cherries or fresh grapes
kala namak and bhuna jeera to taste

1. Boil 3 cups water with 1 tsp salt and a pinch of haldi. Add babycorns and boil for 3-4 minutes till soft. Remove from water. Cut into 2 pieces. Wipe dry and put in a bowl. Add ½ tsp salt, vinegar, olive oil and coriander or parsley. Mix well. Keep aside for atleast 10 minutes or more in fridge.
2. Sprinkle kala namak and bhuna jeera on the pineapple.
3. Push through a tooth pick - a cherry, cheese, mint leaf, baby corn, pineapple and end with a mint leaf. Make more sticks. Serve chilled.

SNACKY DINNER

Quick unfried Dahivada

Prepare at least one hour before serving, for the bread to soak the dahi.

Serves 4-6   *cal/portion 96*

2 slices of fresh bread, preferably whole wheat bread
1½ cups thick curd (of toned milk) - beat till smooth
½ tsp bhuna jeera powder (roasted cumin powder)
½ tsp red chilli powder
1 tbsp finely chopped fresh coriander
¼ tsp kala namak
3/4 tsp salt, or to taste

CHUTNEY

1 tbsp amchoor (dry mango powder)
3 tbsp sugar
¼ tsp red chilli powder
¼ tsp garam masala
¼ tsp bhuna jeera powder (roasted cumin powder)
salt to taste

1. Whip curd. Mix all spices and fresh coriander to get a raita.
2. Cut sides of bread and arrange in a shallow dish.
3. Pour the dahi on it to cover completely. Let the dahi cover the empty spaces of the dish also.
4. Sprinkle red chilli powder and bhuna jeera powder on the dahi.
5. With a spoon, pour the chutney on it, in circles.
6. Garnish with bhuna jeera, red chilli powder and fresh coriander.
7. Leave in the fridge for atleast ½ hour for the bread to soak the curd.
8. Serve with extra chutney.

Note: Although these are not individual pieces of dahi badas, it tastes very much like dahi badas. I am positive you will like it!

Indian chana Pizza

There are days when there are leftovers of a meal in the fridge. For e.g. a bowl of chhole, so here is an innovative idea. Ready-made kulchas are topped with home made chhole- bhature's channas and grilled.

Serves 6   *cal/portion 136*

4 ready made kulchas
1 cups leftover chhole (safed channe)
4 tbsp mango chutney, ready made or home made
1 onion - cut into rings
1 tbsp chopped coriander
salt to taste
½ cup grated paneer

1. Spread 1 tbsp of mango chutney on a kulcha.
2. Spread some onion rings on it.
3. Heat the channas separately in a pan. Spread 2 tbsp of hot channas on the mango chutney kulcha.
4. Sprinkle some coriander and salt on it.
5. Sprinkle some grated paneer on it.
6. Grill or bake for about 15 minutes at 180°C or till the kulcha gets crisp. Do not over grill, it turns hard. Cut into small triangular pieces and serve hot.

Mango chutney Footlong

Serves 8   *cal/portion 97*

1 long garlic bread - cut lengthwise to get 2 thin, long pieces
½ tbsp butter - softened
2 tbsp sweet mango chutney (fun food)
1 kheera - cut into round slices without peeling
2 firm tomatoes - cut into round slices
400 gm paneer - cut into ¼" thick round slices with a kulfi mould cover
few poodina (mint) leaves to garnish - dipped in chilled water
1 tbsp oil

SPRINKLE ON PANEER

¼ tsp haldi, ½ tsp chilli powder, ½ tsp salt, 1 tsp chaat masala powder

1. Spread butter very lightly on the cut surface of both the piece of garlic bread.
2. Place the garlic bread in the oven at 200°C on a wire rack for 10-12 minutes till crisp and light brown on the cut surface. Keep aside.

3. Cut paneer into ¼" thick slices and then cut the slices into round pieces with a kulfi mould (saancha) cover or a biscuit cutter. You can cut the paneer into 1½" square pieces also.

4. Sprinkle the paneer on both sides with some chilli powder, salt, haldi and chaat masala.

5. At serving time, heat 1 tbsp oil in a non stick pan. Saute paneer pieces in the pan on both sides till slightly toasted to a nice yellowish-brown colour. Keep aside.

6. To assemble the footlong, apply 1 tbsp mango chutney on each garlic bread.

7. Sprinkle some chaat masala on the kheera and tomato pieces. Sprinkle some chat masala on the paneer also.

8. Place a piece of paneer, then kheera, then tomato and keep repeating all three in the same sequence so as to cover the loaf. Keep paneer, kheera and tomato, slightly overlapping. Insert fresh mint leaves in between the vegetables, so that they show. Serve.

Note: Mango chutney is available in bottles in stores.

Lebanese smoked Sandwich

Picture on page 103   Serves 4   cal/portion 92

2 Lebanese bread or pita bread or pizza base

75 gms paneer - cut into 1" rectangular pieces of ½" thickness (¾ cup pieces)

1 capsicum, same melted butter

125 gm big mushrooms (4-5), 1 tomato

½ tsp freshly crushed pepper, ½ tsp oregano, ¾ tsp salt

4 tbsp curd - well beaten

1. Wash capsicum, mushrooms and tomato. Pat dry on a clean cloth. Rub melted butter on them all over. Insert a fork or a knife on to the greased capsicum. Roast on a naked flame, turning sides, directly on the heat till charred (slightly blackened) from various sides. Roast for 2-3 minutes. Cool. Chop the smoked capsicum.  Roast the mushrooms and tomato also in the same way on a naked flame. Chop both finely.   *Contd...*

Baked Chick Pea Rounds : Recipe on page 12 ➤

2. Roast paneer also in the same way on the naked flame with forks or tongs. To hasten the process you can use 4 forks on the same flame at the same time.
3. Mix all the smoked ingredients together in a bowl. Add pepper, oregano and ¼ tsp salt. Mix well.
4. Open up the Lebanese bread from one side, like a pocket. On each pita bread or Lebanese bread spread inside the bread ½ of the curd mixture. Spread on just one side.
5. Spread ½ of the roasted vegetable mixture on the curd mixture.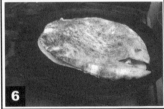
6. Keep on a hot pan or tawa and cook for about 2-3 minutes on both sides. Cut into four triangular. Serve hot.

◅ *Mushroom Croustades : Recipe on page 96*

Mushroom Croustades

Picture on page 94   *Serves 2*   *cal/portion 42*

2 hot dog buns
FILLING
9-10 mushrooms (120 gms) - chopped finely, 1 tsp butter
2 small spring onions (hara pyaz)- chopped till the green
2 tsp veg oyster sauce or soya sauce, ½ tsp salt, ½ tsp pepper or to taste

1. Cut one hot dog bun in half lengthwise. Scoop out the soft middle with a knife, leaving a border. Cut both the pieces further into 2 pieces.
2. Grill all the 4 pieces in a preheated oven till crisp.
3. For the filling, heat butter in a pan, add white of spring onions. Cook till golden. Add mushrooms, cook for 3-4 minutes or till dry.
4. Add soya sauce, salt and pepper. Add greens of spring onion. Mix. Remove from fire.
5. Spoon this mixture into grilled hollowed bread croustades and serve.

CHUTNEYS & DIPS

Light mustard Dip

Picture on cover   *Serves 4*   *cal/portion 3*

4 tsp prepared mustard (English mustard paste), approx.
5 tbsp curd - beat till smooth, ¼ tsp salt, ¼ tsp freshly ground pepper, or to taste

1. Beat all the ingredients together until thick and creamy. Add more mustard, if required to get a nice yellow colour. Check the salt.
2. Refrigerate for about 1 hour.
3. Serve garnished with a mint sprig, with any snacks or carrot, cucumber or celery sticks.

Meethi chutney

Serves 6   *cal/portion 20*

1 tbsp amchoor (dried mango powder), 2 tbsp sugar or shakkar (gur)
½ tsp roasted jeera (cumin seeds), ¼ tsp red chilli powder
¼ tsp salt, ¼ tsp garam masala, ¼ cup water
2-3 pinches of saunth (dry ginger powder), optional

1. Mix all ingredients together in a small heavy bottomed pan.
2. Cook on low flame, till all the ingredients dissolve properly and the chutney gets the right consistency. Remove from fire.

Hari Chutney

cal/portion 13   *Serves 6*   *Picture on cover*

½ cup poodina leaves (½ bunch)
1 cup hara dhania (coriander) - chopped along with the stem
2 green chillies - chopped
2-3 flakes garlic - chopped finely
1 onion - chopped
1 tbsp lemon juice, or to taste
1½ tsp sugar, ½ tsp salt, a pinch of black salt (kala namak)

1. Wash coriander and mint leaves.
2. Grind all ingredients with just enough water to get the right chutney consistency.

Lahsun ki Chutney

Serves 8   *cal/portion 19*

15 flakes garlic - finely chopped
4-5 dry red chillies
1 tsp saboot dhania, 1 tsp jeera, 1 tbsp oil
½ tsp salt, 1 tsp sugar
2 tbsp lemon juice, or to taste

1. Break the stem of the red chillies and break into small pieces. Remove the seeds by tapping the chillies. Soak in 4-5 tbsp hot water for ½ hour.
2. For the chutney, grind the soaked chillies along with the water, garlic, dhania, jeera, oil and sugar and lemon juice to a semi-smooth paste.
3. Heat 1 tbsp oil and cook for 2 minutes on low heat or till oil separates. Add ¼ cup water and bring to a boil. Simmer for 2 minutes. Remove from fire.

Dahi poodina Chutney

cal/portion 18   *Serves 6*

GRIND TOGETHER
½ cup poodina (mint), ½ cup hara dhania (green coriander)
2 green chillies
½ onion, 2 flakes garlic

ADD LATER
1½ cups curd - hang for 15 minutes
a pinch of kala namak, ¼ tsp bhuna jeera, salt to taste
1 tsp oil

1. Hang curd in a muslin cloth for 15 minutes. Keep aside.
2. Wash coriander and mint leaves.
3. Grind coriander, mint, green chillies, onion and garlic with a little water to a paste.
4. Beat hung curd well till smooth.
5. To the hung curd, add the green paste, oil, kala namak, bhuna jeera and salt to taste.

Minty strawberry Dip

Serves 8   *cal/portion 20*

3 cups curd (of toned milk) - hung in a muslin cloth for 1 hour
3/4 cup chopped strawberries
¼ cup chopped mint
¼ tsp sugar, salt to taste

TO SERVE WITH
vegetable sticks of carrots, cucumber or blanched broccoli florets

1. Tie the yogurt in a muslin cloth and hang it to drain for 1 hour. 3 cups yogurt will give about 1½ cups hung yogurt.
2. Blend strawberries for a few seconds to make a strawberry puree.
3. Beat the yogurt till smooth.
4. Mix strawberry puree, mint, salt & sugar to the beaten yogurt. Chill.
5. Serve with peeled carrot and cucumber cut into sticks and blanched broccoli florets with long stalks.

Lebanese Smoked Sandwich : Recipe on page 92 ➢

BEST SELLERS BY  SNAB
Excellence in Books

Biryanis & Pulaos

Baking Recipes

Baby Cookbook

Microwave Cakes & Snacks

Diet Snacks & Desserts

Drinks & Indian Desserts

Indian Favourites Vegetarian

Lebanese Recipes

Pasta Recipes Vegetarian

Sandwiches & Wraps

Paranthas & Rice for Kids

Recipes for Growing Kids